SHARKY MALARKEY

A SKETCHSHARK COLLECTION

SHARKY MALARKEY

A SKETCHSHARK COLLECTION

MEGAN NICOLE DONG

Andrews McMeel
PUBLISHING®

8

 MY NAME is
MEGAN

 AND I
AM...

A CARTOONIST

I AM A
CAT OWNER

(THIS PLUMP CREATURE'S
NAME IS CHAOS)

13

14

...I AM A CAT OWNER

WHO ALSO HAS CAT ALLERGIES

SNUFF
SNUFF
SNIRFF

STANDARD STRESS RATING
SCALE

1 —— 2 —— 3 —— 4

NO
STRESS

MILD
CONCERN

THERE IS A
SMOKE DETECTOR
CHIRPING
NEARBY, BUT
it is UNCLEAR
WHICH ONE
it is.

A SMOKE
DETECTOR
is RIGHT
NEAR THE
PLACE
WHERE THE
COOKING
HAPPENS.

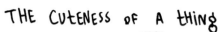

THE CUTENESS OF A THING

IS DIRECTLY PROPORTIONAL to the UGLINESS OF THE FACE I MAKE WHEN LOOKING AT it.

CHAPTER 1

MALARKEY

How to Cope with a Busy Schedule

GET ORGANIZED

STRESS CHEESE

EXERCISE

STRESS CHEESE

PET AN ANIMAL

STRESS. CHEESE.

LISTEN TO CLASSICAL MUSI-

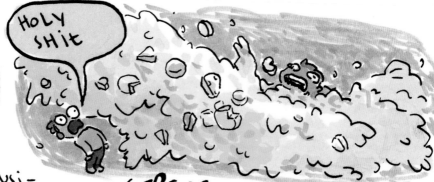

HOLY SHIT

STREEEHHSSS CHEÉÉEEEZZE

WOKE UP
too LATE

CANNOT FIND
KEYS

FEEL
FEEL
FEEL

HORSES ARE JUDGING ME

turn

THE PRIMARY CAUSES
of ANXIETY

WORK STRESS

Berate Berate

Family/Friend Drama

WONDERING what PEOPLE think of me

WONDERING...What if there is a BEAR SECRETLY Living in my apartment

Shake Friend Shake

But I can't PROVE THE BEAR EXISTS to anyone ELSE

AND WHEN I DO finally see the BEAR

It JUST looks me in the EYE

and SCREAMS

HOMEOWNER PROBLEMS

LEAKY ROOFS

DRAFTY WINDOWS

AN INFESTATION
OF SHYBOYS

BLACK MOLD

SHYBOYS. SHYBOYS IN THE WALLS.
SHYBOYS IN THE CEILING...

GODDAMN. SOMEBODY THROW A PARTY SO WE CAN BE RID OF
THESE FREELOADING SHYBOYS.

DYNAMIC JERRY

A MAN WAS WALKING TO THE BUS STOP WHEN HE ENCOUNTERED AN OLD BEGGAR WOMAN...

SOME SHELTER FOR A SINGLE ROSE?

...UM... NO.

THE BEGGAR WOMAN TRANSFORMED INTO A BEAUTIFUL ENCHANTRESS

OH SHIT.

FROM THIS DAY FORTH YOU WILL ONLY BE ABLE TO POOP AT WORK!!

NOOOOOOO

CURSE

40

EVERYBODY DESERVES A SPECIAL SOMEONE

SOMEONE to HOLD YOUR HAND WHEN YOU NEED REASSURANCE

SOMEONE to LISTEN to YOUR FEARS AND YOUR WOES

...I HAVE So many...

SOMEONE to STARE AT YOU WITH ITS giant goat-EYE

WAIT....

SOMEONE to CARESS YOUR HAIR WITH ITS MANY FACE-TENTACLES.

OH GOD, NO.

SOMEONE to PURSUE YOU WITH ITS MANY BIRD-FEET

SOMEONE WHO CAN'T WAIT to INTRODUCE YOU to its PARENTS WHEN It ABDUCTS YOU to its PARALLEL-CHAOS-UNIVERSE HOME

HMM HMMM

SHiiiIt

MY ONLY WISH

is to SPACE OUT IN YOUR DIRECTION

WHILE YOU SPACE OUT IN MY DIRECTION...

WHILE THE PETS SPACE OUT AT EACH OTHER

...ALL OF US JUST SPACING IN THE SAME SPACE...

AVERAGE guys with PERKY BUNS

45

46

48

49

COMMON UNCOMFORTABLE SITUATIONS

Walking alongside a friend after hugging them goodbye

Responding to a basic query incorrectly

How are you?

Yes.

Finding out that your boyfriend has secretly been bees all this time

COMPLIMENTS

CONFIDENT PEOPLE

Takes Pride in Fashion Choices

Is Never Fazed By Exams

Will Eat Spoonfuls of Condiments in Front of Anybody

TERRIBLE College FURNITURESTUFFS

Gristly Futon

CHAir MaDE OF
STAPLED ParticleBoaRD

BeanBag chair
that REQUIRES
a LitterBox

Lamp that BELIEVES
that you are its
tHeraPist

THE TRAGIC TALE OF THE PUNMAKER

NEIGHBORS WHO SOMEHOW LIVE IN EVERY APARTMENT BUILDING YOU'VE EVER KNOWN

JUDGY LADY LOBBYING TO CUT DOWN EVERY TENANT'S PRIVACY TREES

GUY WHO FREQUENTLY TRIES TO INVITE YOU OVER TO SEE HIS COLLECTION OF too MANY LIZARDS

AMBIGUOUSLY PREJUDICED GRANDPA-TYPE WHO ONLY REFERS TO PEOPLE BY THE DEMOGRAPHIC GROUPS to WHICH THEY BELONG

EACH OTHER'S

CES

THINKING ABOUT CUTE BOYS

THINKING ABOUT CUTE LADIES

THINKING ABOUT ANY DOG

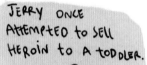

A

SIMPLY DRAWN

MAN

JUST a
SIMPLY DRAWN
MAN

WITH BEAUTIFULLY
DRAWN EYES

MY MOUTH is
JUST A LINE

MY tEEtH
ARE
PHoto-REALiStic

YES I'M A
SIMPLY DRAWN
MAN

WITH A SIMPLY
DRAWN ASS

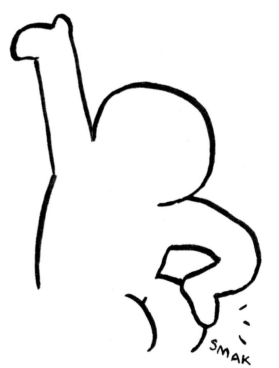

SMAK

A MAN THINKS ABOUT HIS GOALS

A MAN THINKS ABOUT PAST LOVES

A MAN THINKS ABOUT WHAT THE DOCTOR WARNED HIM WOULD HAPPEN IF HE BECAME TOO SELF-REFLECTIVE

A MAN—

CHAPTER 2
THERE'S A
SHARK
IN LOS ANGELES

BRUC

SASSM: You came into cultural prominence in the '70s when you starred in a film that became a classic.
Bruce: Indeed I did.

SASSM: The film had a lasting cultural impact . . .
Bruce: Mmm, yes.

SASSM: . . . by misrepresenting sharks as murderous, man-eating beasts. Do you regret your role in perpetuating stereotypes about your own kind? Stereotypes so horrible they led to the unnecessary slaughter of great white sharks worldwide?
Bruce: . . . No? Is that weird?

SASSM: It's kind of weir—
Bruce: Listen, before you get all uppity—we were nominated for Oscars. I . . . got to go to the Oscars. I mean . . . You understand, right?

SASSM: I don't get it . . . really. We did research. Several of your blood relatives were killed. CLOSE blood relatives, like first cousins and a sister of yours were killed because of anti-shark hysteria drummed up by the movie you starred in. Don't you feel ANY remorse at all?
Bruce: . . . (absentmindedly humming a medley of Bette Midler ballads) Sorry . . . what was that?

SASSM: Did you not hear my question?
Bruce: My brain heard some of it, but my heart did not.

SASSM: God. Nevermind . . . Our readers are only here for fluff and tawdry gossip, anyway. Can you tell us something we don't know about you?

Bruce: Hmm . . . My name isn't actually Bruce. It's actually Jonathan. The movie crew knew a guy—a human guy named Bruce who looked a lot like me. So. Y'know. Here we are.

SASSM: So you didn't, like, legally change your name or anything? You just never corrected them? For decades?
Jonathan: Neehhhh.

SASSM: . . . Anyway, it's been over 40 years since your one successful film. That is a long time. What have you been up to since then?
Jonathan: Social. Media. Baby. Not to be a braggart or anything, but I have nearly 900 followers on what the teens call "the Grams." Gotta love social media. Gotta love those teens.

SASSM: Gross. Anyway, what do you post on social media?
Jonathan: All selfies. Most of them of the lower-back, upper-ass-crack region. Do you want to see?

SASSM: N . . . no. No thank y—
Jonathan: HERE.

SASSM: Oh wow . . . You weren't lying. This is mostly asses.
Jonathan: I'm EXTREMELY proud of my upper ass. I have hired a personal trainer to help me focus exclusively on that region of my body. Do you want to see videos of it flexing? It's like a 90-minute video; you'll love i—

SASSM: I have no more questions. You are a terrible person.
Jonathan: Well, technically, I'm not a person. I'm a shark, you IDIOT.

Holy Shit, I'm So FANCY

Hop

CLOMP

HUP

Stomp

WORKING ON HEALTH

WORKING ON SELF-ESTEEM

WORKING ON MENTAL STRENGTH

WORKING ON TIME MANAGEMENT

COMMON HOBBIES

UNNECESSARY
BROWSING

OVEREATING

REMEMBERING
EMBARRASSING
MOMENTS FROM
YEARS AGO

YELLING AT NOTHING

DOES it MAKE YOU
UNCOMFORTABLE WHEN
I STARE LIKE this?

ASSHOLE FACES

84

85

are you jealous?

you fucking should be.

FULL OF SECREt Bitchyfeelings

100

TOO TiReD to FUNCTION

Too AWAKE to Stop FiXATiNG oN DEATH

FEELING CONFIDENT

FEELING SHY

FEELING CONFIDENT

...BUT STILL KIND OF SHY

STRAAATCH

REST

Bury

your

Feelings

8 EASY Life tips for Ladies who want that Healthy glow!!

Take a yoga class!

Go on a Juice cleanse!

Laugh with a salad

Start a cult

Laugh with a salad made by vegetables grown by your cult

Try a mud mask!

Start a second cult

Laugh with a salad and juice while your cults battle to the death to win your favor

JUST AN AMBITIOUS, BRIGHT-EYED, SUBURBAN COLLEGE GRAD

Walking to HER First JOB in THE Big city

GETTING HARASSED BY a MAN IN a DUMPSTER

PASSING USED PREGNANCY TESTS ON THE SIDEWALK

WATCHING CUTE BIRDS...

BATHE IN HUMAN PEE

BAAARB

HOW I WOULD ADVERTISE LASH-STRENGTHENING MASCARA

NAIL TRENDS

FRENCH TIPS

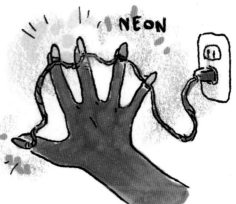

NEON

TURKEY - TAIL NAILS

Rattle Rattle Rattle Skkrnt! Rattle Rattle Rattle

FAN NAIL

SKYSCRAPER STYLE

NAIL-IN-A-NAIL-IN-A-NAIL ARt

REAL GIRLS TALK REAL BODY INSECURITIES

I THINK MY THIGHS ARE TOO BIG!

LISA

MY SKIN BREAKS OUT ALL THE TIME!

KATE

MY MOUTH IS ALSO MY ANUS!!

JELLYFISH

M...MY ARMS ARE TOO LONG?

SACHA

GYAAAH

SACHA

MY ARMS ARE FULL OF VENOM... I DESPERATELY DESIRE FRIENDSHIP, BUT MY HUGS CAUSE DEATH.

A TYPE-A TEEN GETS HER FIRST JOB

graceful

CLip
CLoP

CLoMP

CLup

CLiPPA
CLoP

CLiPPity
CLoPPity

CLuMPA CLoPPLE
CLoP

CLuP
CLoP

THEY ARE THE ARMS NOW

130

131

Things Other Humans May Say to You When You Go Outside Without Makeup

ARE YOU CERTAIN THAT YOU
DON'T WANT TO MAKE CHILDRENS??

A MOMENT WITH A MAN WHO HAS UNREALISTIC EXPECTATIONS

135

It's **BROWN BEARD BLUE EYES**

THE HOT, SEXY DATING SHOW WHEREIN ONE DRUNK WOMAN IS DRUNKENLY COURTED BY A SWARM OF BROWN-BEARDED, BLUE-EYED MEN WHO ARE ALSO SO DRUNK

MEET OUR MEN

CHASE
ENJOYS READING A GOOD SOUP CAN LABEL

DASE
IS CURRENTLY PURSUING A MASTER'S IN SNOWMEN

TROSTYN
HIS FAVORITE HOBBY IS GOING TO HIS LOCAL JCPENNEY TO NEG THE MANNEQUINS

DRENT
DREAMS OF ONE DAY CLEANSING THE WORLD OF BIRDS

ZESTER
HAS ONLY HAD SEX WITH RACISTS

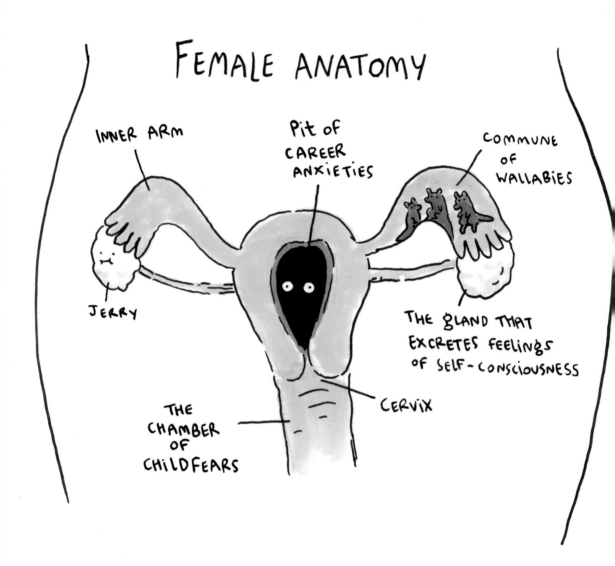

FEMALE ANATOMY

INNER ARM

Pit of CAREER ANXIETIES

COMMUNE OF WALLABIES

JERRY

THE GLAND THAT EXCRETES FEELINGS OF SELF-CONSCIOUSNESS

CERVIX

THE CHAMBER OF CHILDFEARS

Menstruation & You

YOUR BODY IS CHANGING!

SOME WOMEN EXPERIENCE UTERINE CRAMPING!

SOME WOMEN HAVE MOOD SWINGS AND TEMPORARY ACNE

SOME WOMEN HAVE FREQUENT POOPS

SOME WOMEN DEVELOP RODENTKINESIS

SOME WOMEN'S BODIES BECOME GATEWAYS TO PARALLEL DIMENSIONS INHABITED BY BEINGS SO UNKNOWABLE THE MERE SIGHT OF THEM WILL DRIVE A PERSON MAD

AND NOW, A MOMENT WITH SOME MEN WHO HAVE BEEN DECEIVED BY MAKEUP

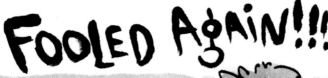

143

THE HEART OF
A LION

THE STRENGTH
OF AN
OX

THE FACE OF
A BUDGIE

turn

FWAP
FWP
FWAPP

CHAPTER 4

THE ANIMALS + PLANTS CHANNEL

ALL PROGRAMMING ON THE ANIMALS + PLANTS CHANNEL™ IS BROUGHT TO YOU BY OUR SPONSOR PETROL-LA-LA! CORP.

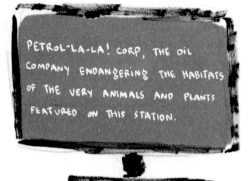

PETROL-LA-LA! CORP, THE OIL COMPANY ENDANGERING THE HABITATS OF THE VERY ANIMALS AND PLANTS FEATURED ON THIS STATION.

PETROL-LA-LA! CORP. WE DON'T UNDERSTAND THIS PARTNERSHIP EITHER.

THE PEACH TREE HAS PINK FLOWERS IN SPRINGTIME...

It BEARS NECTARINES AND PEACH FRUIT.

It HAS A BODY tHAt JUST WON'T QUIT.

How to SASS

NOT ENOUGH.

TOO FAR. THE WORLD IS NOT READY.

YES.

THE PROPHET CLAM'S VISION

A SELECTION OF NORTH AMERICAN FAUNA

THE GREAT HORNED OWL

THE COMMON RACCOON

THE SECRETLY RACIST FIELD MOUSE

CONDESCENDING DEER

IMMODEST FROGS

PURGE BIRDS

SQUIRRELS YOU MAY ENCOUNTER

GRAY SQUIRREL

FOX SQUIRREL

NORTHERN FLYING SQUIRREL

EASTERN PENNY-FARTHING SQUIRREL

TALL SQUIRREL

MAGICAL SQUIRREL

STREET-PREACHING SQUIRREL

JEFFREY

WE DO NOT TALK ABOUT JEFFREY.

Whale Anatomy

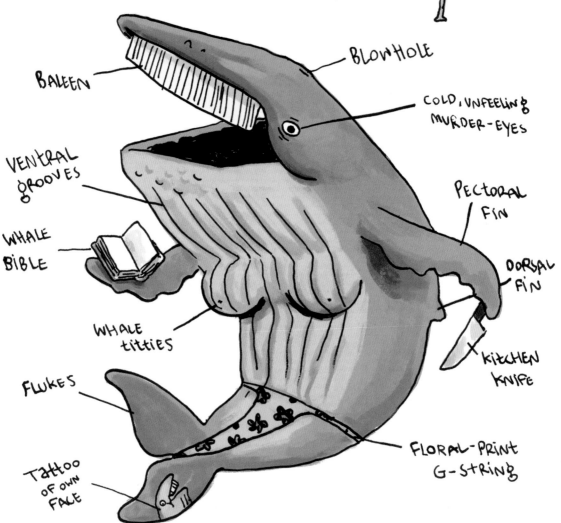

BLOWHOLE

BALEEN

COLD, UNFEELING MURDER-EYES

VENTRAL GROOVES

WHALE BIBLE

PECTORAL FIN

DORSAL FIN

WHALE titties

KITCHEN KNIFE

FLUKES

FLORAL-PRINT G-STRING

Tattoo OF OWN FACE

TERRESTRIAL LOCOMOTION

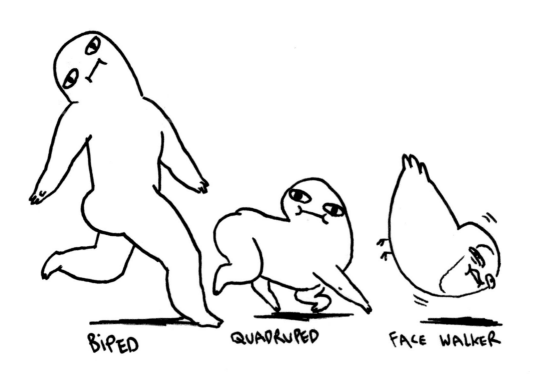

BIPED   QUADRUPED   FACE WALKER

CARNIVOROUS PLANTS of the WORLD

VENUS FLYTRAP

PITCHER PLANT

SUNDEW

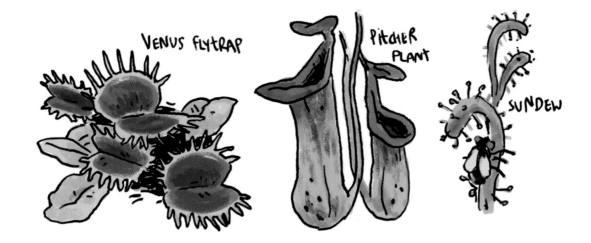

POSSESSED PINE TREES

Tortoises vs. Turtles

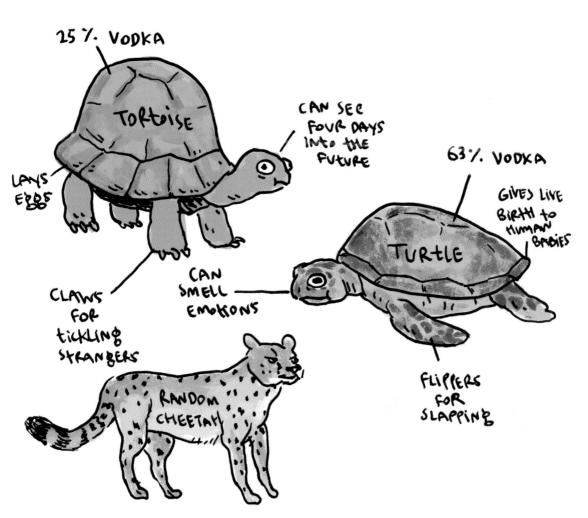

25% VODKA

TORTOISE

CAN SEE FOUR DAYS INTO THE FUTURE

LAYS EGGS

CLAWS FOR tickling STRANGERS

CAN SMELL EMOTIONS

63% VODKA

GIVES LIVE BIRTH to HUMAN BABIES

TURTLE

FLIPPERS FOR SLAPPING

RANDOM CHEETAH

A DOLPHIN

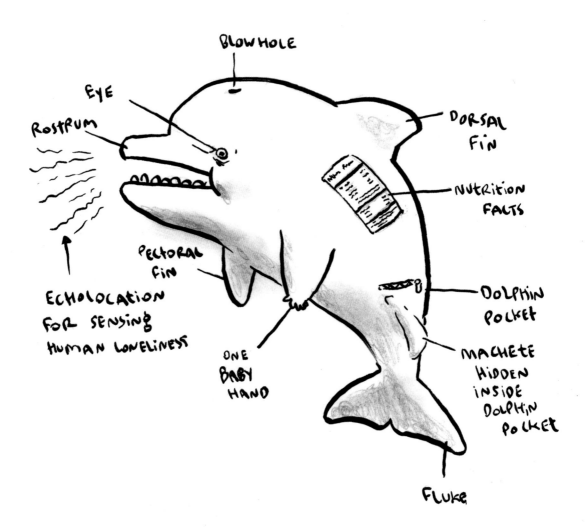

BLOWHOLE

EYE

ROSTRUM

DORSAL FIN

NUTRITION FACTS

PECTORAL FIN

ECHOLOCATION FOR SENSING HUMAN LONELINESS

DOLPHIN POCKET

ONE BABY HAND

MACHETE HIDDEN INSIDE DOLPHIN POCKET

FLUKE

Hot Snails

HOW THE ANIMALS HIDE

BiRD Courtship Rituals

Local Pest Animals

Roof Rat

Feral Pigeon

Murder Pony

Satanic Goldfish

Multilevel-Marketing Marmots

WILDLIFE in DISTRESS

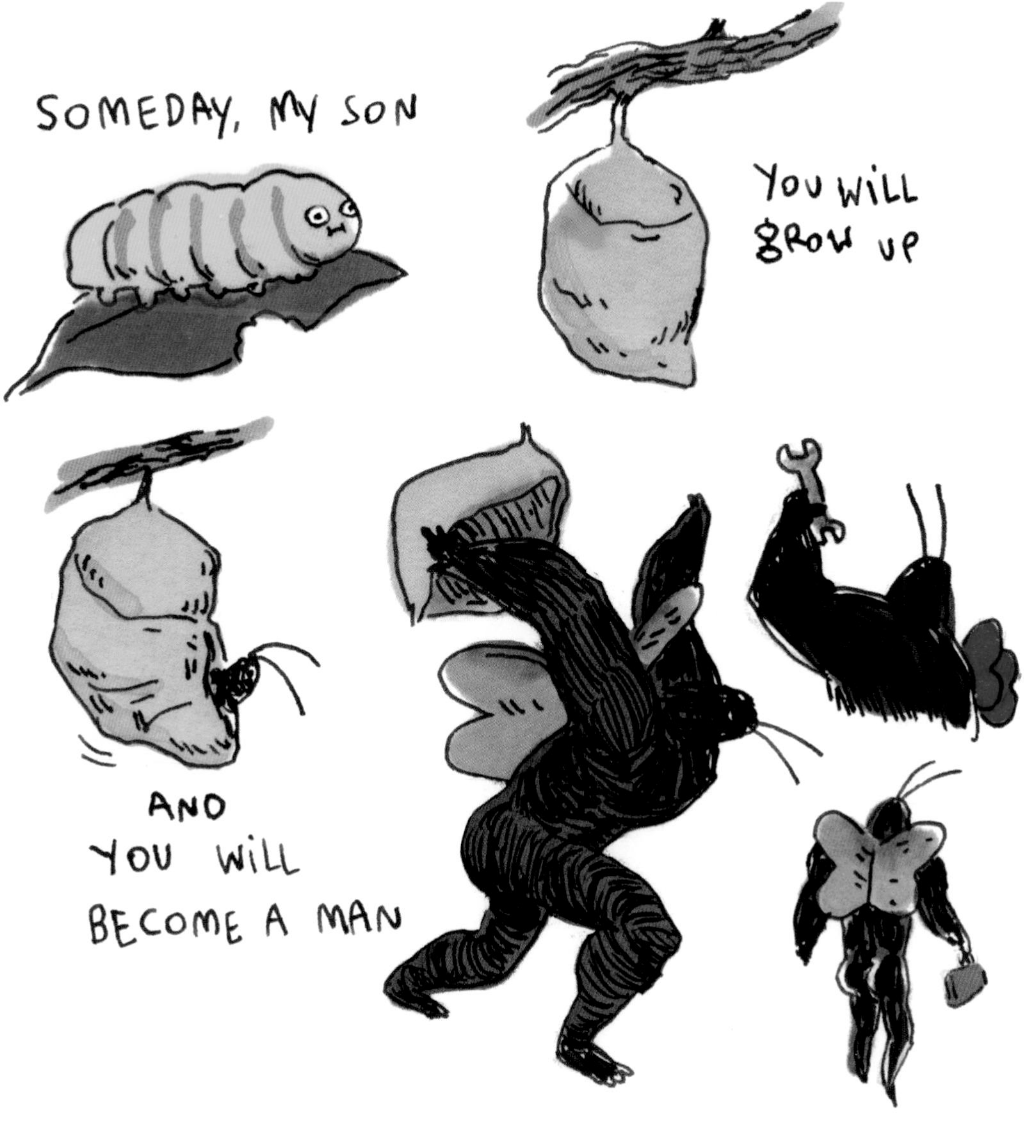
SOMEDAY, MY SON
YOU WILL GROW UP
AND YOU WILL BECOME A MAN

Santa's Reindeer

SASSER

LUMPISH

BONGER

SPLITENDS

SCOOTY

BiG-BALLS

A GREYHOUND

PiGEON

RONALPH

I'VE SEEN SOME SHit

THE QUARTER CENTAURS

3/4 MAN, 1/4 HORSE

3/4 HORSE, 1/4 MAN

THE BEARPORT

WILDLIFE PHOTOGRAPHY WORST-SELLERS

MORE SELECTIONS FROM tHE WiLDLiFE PHOTOGRAPHY BARGAiN BiN

WILDLIFE PHOTOGRAPHY WORST-SELLERS 3

SERVICE ANIMALS FOR iNTERNET-AVERSE ADULTS

A CAT THAT CURATES VIDEOS OF OTHER CATS

THE ACRONYM OWL

A GOAT THAT UNDERSTANDS MEMES

A BOX TORTOISE THAT ONLY SAYS "YAAAS"

THE DANGEROUS ANIMALS

THE HIPPOPOTAMUS

THE SEA
WASP

THE REEF
STONEFISH

THE LOW-BUDGET
CGI BIRD WITH
EERILY SERENE
EYES

SWOOP

STEAL

EXAMPLES OF
CETACEAN SURFACING BEHAVIOR

ORCA SPYHOPPING

HUMPBACK WHALE TAIL SLAPPING

CALIFORNIA GRAY WHALE MOCKING SEA BIRDS

DOLPHINS THAT ARE TRYING JUST WAY TOO HARD RIGHT NOW

MORE COMMON KINDS OF SHARK ATTACKS

ATTENDING YOUR WEDDING

IN A WHITE-ASS DRESS

IGNORING THE HELL OUT OF YOUR HAIRCUT

BLAMING YOU FOR THE WEIRD SMELL IN THE OFFICE

TURNING ON READ RECEIPTS

JUST SO YOU CAN SEE YOUR TEXTS ARE UNIMPORTANT

ASKING TO BORROW A CIGARETTE AND A LIGHT

AND THEN SETTING YOUR CAR ON FIRE

CHAPTER 5

A TOAD MAKES NEW FRIENDS IN THE FOREST

ON A COOL AUTUMN MORNING, A LONE TADPOLE
HATCHED IN
A SHALLOW CREEK.

ALL OF ITS SIBLINGS HAD BEEN EATEN BY CRAYFISH,
ITS PARENTS ALSO EATEN (BY A DUCK)...

BUT THE PLUCKY LITTLE TADPOLE SURVIVED.

It GREW AND GREW; its taiL SHRIVELED AWAY,

AND its BODY SPROUTED tiny LimBS.

ONE DAY, tHE tADPOLE SAt UP ABOVE tHE WAtERLiNE,
PEERED DOWN At its REFLECtiON,

AND SAW tHAt it HAD BECOME A toAD.

LIFE IN THE CREEK WAS LONELY, AND THE THREAT OF DUCKS AND CRAYFISH LOOMED IN THE TOAD'S INCREDIBLY FREQUENT NIGHTMARES.

But most of ALL,

THE TOAD CRAVED FRIENDSHIP.

PACKING NOTHING, BECAUSE THE GODDAMN CRAYFISH HAD RAIDED ITS FOOD STORES THE MORNING PRIOR, THE TOAD DECIDED TO LEAVE ITS WATERY HOME AND VENTURE OFF TO THE BIG FOREST.

HE FOREST WAS BUSTLING WITH ANIMALS LARGE AND SMALL. MOST OF THEM HAD NEVER ENCOUNTERED A TOAD BEFORE.

GIDDY WITH EXCITEMENT, THE TOAD HAPPILY SET
OFF TO MEET ALL OF ITS NEW NEIGHBORS.

210

CHAPTER 6
SOME SORT OF END

♪ IN a MULTICOLORED HAZE

♫ IF YOU DREAM

YOU CAN

DO ANYTHING ♪

♫ LIKE DEFY THE laws of PHYSICS and THE PROBLEMS of SocieTal inEQuality

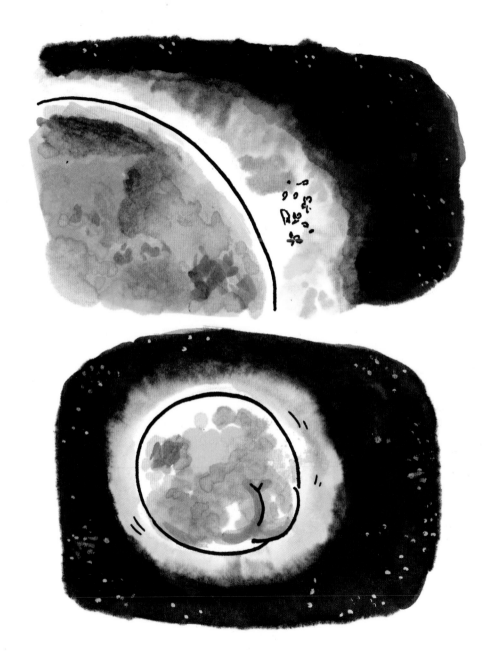

SPECIAL THANKS to STUART LIVINGSTON, MONICA DONG, ERWIN LEDFORD, AMINDER DHALIWAL, AND MAHA TABIKH. THANK YOU to ALLISON ADLER, MELISSA RHODES, AND ANDREWS MCMEEL. ALL OF YOU ARE WONDERFUL AND I COULD NOT HAVE MADE THIS SILLY BOOK WITHOUT YOUR HELP, GUIDANCE, AND ENCOURAGEMENT.

Andrews McMeel Publishing
a division of Andrews McMeel Universal
1130 Walnut Street, Kansas City, Missouri 64106

www.andrewsmcmeel.com
www.instagram.com/sketchshark

18 19 20 21 22 TEN 10 9 8 7 6 5 4 3 2 1

ISBN: 978-1-4494-8755-3

Library of Congress Control Number: 2017962387

Editor: Allison Adler
Art Director: Spencer Williams
Production Editor: Elizabeth A. Garcia
Production Manager: Tamara Haus

ATTENTION: SCHOOLS AND BUSINESSES

Andrews McMeel books are available at quantity discounts with bulk purchase for educational, business, or sales promotional use. For information, please e-mail the Andrews McMeel Publishing Special Sales Department: specialsales@amuniversal.com.